Contents

Get fit!

You only have one body – so it's up to you to look after it. Getting active is the best way to keep yourself happy and healthy. Just go for it!

Couch potato

Do you watch too much TV? Make a note every day of how long you sit in front of the telly. After a week, look back at how many hours you spent – is it time to cut back and do something more active instead?

Computer crazy?

Surfing the web and playing computer games don't give your muscles much of a workout! Take regular breaks and listen to your mum or dad if they nag you to hop up and do something else!

Take it outside!

Fix a time to meet your friends after school – why not use up some energy skating around the park or shooting hoops at the local basketball court? Don't forget to tell someone at home where you're going and when you'll be back.

Stretch your legs

Look for new ways to make exercise part of your everyday life. If you have an older brother or sister, ask them to walk to school with you instead of getting a lift. If you live too far away, ask your parents to park the car nearby and stride the last part of the journey.

Brilliant biking

Cycling is a super-quick way to get about! If you are not confident at riding yet, go out with your mum or dad a few times first. Always wear a helmet and choose routes that are safe for cycling.

Road safety

If you are walking with friends or riding on your bikes, take care near busy roads. If you are cycling, wear a helmet and make sure that you can be easily seen in the dark.

Move it!

Why not...?

- scooter to the shops
- jog round the block
- ban lifts and take the stairs
- power-walk the dog
- skateboard down the street

Indoor play

Weather not so good? There are still hundreds of indoor sports you can enjoy! Get ready to challenge yourself and share lots of giggles at the same time...

Get together

If you are shy and find it hard to make friends, join a sports club. There are clubs all over the country for every sport you can think of. You could even have some lessons first to help build your confidence.

Fantastic gymnastics

Gymnastics is a cool indoor sport for girls. You can go to gym classes, and there are lots of badges and awards to work for as you improve your skills.

Sky-high

Trampolining keeps you fit and uses up loads of energy. The trick to good bouncing is to get into a rhythm! Learn some awesome moves, then make up your own routine.

Gym basics

Can you crack all six?
1. forward roll
2. handstand
3. backward roll
4. cartwheel
5. headstand
6. hand spring

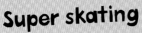

Super skating

Ice-skating is an Olympic sport that can be really competitive. It takes years of hard work to become an ice-skating champ, but there's lots of fun to be had just gliding around your local rink!

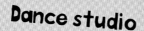

Dance studio

Moving to music will have you working up a sweat in no time! There are so many ways to do it, too. Ballet, tap, jazz, street, Latin and ballroom are all different kinds of dancing.

Watch out!

Martial arts such as judo, ju-jitsu and karate can help keep you both fit and safe. The skills you learn are handy for self-defence. One of the first things you will be taught is how to tumble without hurting yourself.

Splash time

If you can't swim, take the plunge and learn! If you're already pool-confident, work on improving your strokes so that you speed up in the water.

Splashing sports

Give these wicked water sports a try!

- surfing
- canoeing
- waterskiing
- snorkelling
- windsurfing
- rowing

Water baby

Don't worry if all your mates can swim, but you can't. It's never too late to learn! Sign up for beginner's lessons. Some pools even run crash courses to get you swimming quickly.

Choose life

If you can swim already and want a new challenge, why not learn to be a junior life-saver? You learn about water safety, life-saving and how to deal with emergencies.

Keep keen

If you want to race in swimming galas, you'll have to practise hard, but it's well worth the effort! Training usually starts early in the morning, before the school day begins.

Dive in!

If you get a real buzz from diving, it's worth finding a teacher to help you develop your technique. Always check that the water is deep enough to allow you to dive safely.

At sea

If you swim in the sea, make sure you go with an adult. There are currents and washes that could carry even strong swimmers away from the shore. Look out for and obey warning flags, too – they are there to keep you safe.

Pool party

There's so much fun to be had at your local leisure centre! Find out if your pool runs Saturday sessions, work out in a water aerobics class or make up a synchronized swimming routine with your friends.

Outdoor action

Playing sport in the open air works your muscles and gets your heart rate jumping! Winning is also a fab feeling, but nothing beats being part of a great team.

Footie mad

In the UK, more girls play football than netball. So why not join your nearest football club? Be prepared to get muddy when you play!

Anyone for tennis?

Tennis may not be an obvious team game, but if you join a tennis club, you'll make loads of new friends. Doubles matches are always good fun – especially if it's a close game!

Old favourites

Do you play handball, hockey or netball at school? These are all brilliant team sports. When you train, you'll learn tactics as well as improve your co-ordination.

Sophie's Annual Garden Games

Starts 2.00pm, next Saturday

Events: limbo dancing

wheelbarrow racing

toss the welly

assault course

Medal dreams

Can you run faster than your friends, jump higher or throw a ball further across the park? Athletics may be for you! Start training now for a gold medal at the next Olympics, or set up a mini-Games in your back garden.

On the map

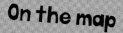

Orienteering is an outdoor activity that gives you tons of fresh air and exercise. You and your pals use a map and compass to find a set of marked spots, before racing back to base. Give it a go!

Work it out

If sport is not your thing, don't say no to all outdoor exercise – just be creative about it! You could try setting up a treasure hunt so you and your pals can run around to find the clues.

Eat smart

You're more likely to keep fit and well if you have a nutritious diet. This means eating healthy meals, saving sweets and treats for special occasions.

Meal deal

You may be a busy bee, but find time to eat three meals a day. Don't skip breakfast, or munch too much between meal times. If you must have a snack, make healthy choices.

Balancing act

There are five key food groups. You should eat some food from each group during the day, eats lots of 1 and 2 and only a little of 4.

1. breads and cereals
2. fruits and vegetables
3. dairy foods
4. sweet and fatty foods
5. meat, fish and eggs

Five a day

Fruits and vegetables are stuffed full of vitamins and minerals which all help your body to work properly. Make a big effort to eat five portions of fruit and vegetables every single day.

Eat up!

Don't forget that smoothies and fruit juice count towards your five-a-day. Don't try to hide the salad and veggies on your plate – eat them all up, including the greens!

Dairy foods

Creamy dairy foods like yoghurt, milk and cheese have calcium in them – a mineral that helps your bones and teeth be strong. Be dairy food-friendly and drink milky drinks whenever you can.

Feeling thirsty?

We all need to eat food, but water is even more important for our survival. You need to drink at least one or two litres of water a day – even more if the weather is hot.

Snack and go

Next time you take sandwiches to school or go on a picnic, pack some new things in your lunchbox! There are all sorts of tasty dips, wraps and snacks to try.

Pack a snack

Next time you're packing for a picnic, ask your mum or dad if you can leave any unhealthy stuff at home. Replace crisps and chocolate with options like fruit, cereal bars and nuts.

Brown is best

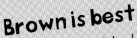

Brown bread is better for you than white bread, because it contains wholemeal grains. Get used to eating brown bread in your sandwiches – and try to eat the crusts, too!

DIY nibbles

Ask if you can bake your own yummy treats. Flapjacks taste great and they are good for you, too! If you make too many to eat by yourself, take some into school to share with your pals. There's a tasty flapjack recipe on page 16.

Mix it up

Always take a bottle of water out with you – it's important to top up your fluid levels throughout the day. If you're tired of plain tap water, add a dash of fruit juice to give it some flavour.

This week's sandwiches

Monday	cream cheese, ham and cucumber
Tuesday	tuna crunch
Wednesday	hummus and grated carrot
Thursday	chicken, chutney and spinach
Friday	prawn mayonnaise

Plan ahead

You'll soon get bored if you always eat the same thing. Experiment with different fillings for your sandwiches, rolls and wraps. Plan a week's lunches, so you eat something different every day.

Shopping list
tin of tuna
baby spinach
red pepper
cream cheese
tortilla wraps

Get involved

Make a list of the healthy snacks that you would like to eat when you're on the go. Talk about the list with your mum and dad, then go shopping together to buy the tasty things you're after.

Get cooking

The best way to learn to cook is to get in the kitchen and help! Watch how your mum or dad prepares food, then pull on an apron and join in.

Baking flapjacks

Make a batch of fruity flapjacks. These scrummy snacks aren't just delicious, they're healthy, too!

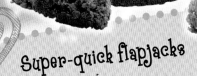

Super-quick flapjacks

You will need:

125g margarine
100g soft dark-brown sugar
60g golden syrup
225g porridge oats
75g dried fruit or nuts*

*Why not add dried sultanas, apricots, coconut or a mix of nuts and seeds?

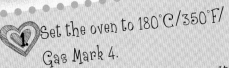
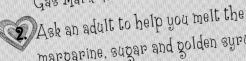
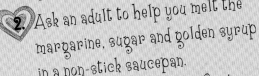

1. Set the oven to 180°C/350°F/ Gas Mark 4.

2. Ask an adult to help you melt the margarine, sugar and golden syrup in a non-stick saucepan.

3. Stir in the oats and dried fruit.

4. Scrape the mixture into a baking tin, then pop it in the oven for half an hour.

5. Take out, let cool and cut into slices!

Cupcake creations

For a special occasion, have a go at baking some cupcakes. When they're cool, whip up some buttercream icing, then sprinkle your cakes with pretty decorations.

Make a menu

When you've had some practice in the kitchen, try cooking a complete meal. Get together with a friend and plan a starter, main course and dessert. Keep things simple the first time around.

Take care in the kitchen. Always ask a grown-up to help you before chopping food or using the oven or hob.

Get organized

Write a list of all the ingredients that you'll need for your meal. Go shopping to buy the stuff, then get cooking!

Dine in style

To make your meal extra special, decorate the kitchen like a posh restaurant, with flowers, napkins and a tablecloth. Write out the menu, so your guests know what dishes to look forward to!

Looking good

It's important to try to look your best, because looking good also makes you feel great. Find your style and get ready to shine!

New style
With long hair, there are all sorts of styles you can try out, but girls with short hair can have fun too! If you have a shorter cut, jazz up your look with clips, gels and funky hair accessories.

Twisty buns
Always brush your hair before you style it to tug out the tangles! Give boring old bunches a makeover by twisting them into messy buns. Try fixing a side bun, or even two high ones at the back.

Plait trick
Wash your hair and tie it into lots of little plaits while it is damp. Leave your hair to dry naturally, then untie the plaits. You'll be left with tumbling, wavy hair!

Fashion exchange

If you're fed up with your wardrobe, don't wait until your next shopping trip. Ask your mum or dad, then revamp your style by swapping clothes with your best friend.

Fashionista wardrobe tips

⭐ organize clothes by colour

⭐ keep your shoes neatly in a rack

⭐ give to charity anything you haven't worn for a year

⭐ pop a fragranced cushion in with socks, tights and pjs

Makeovers and make-up

It is fun to experiment with make-up, but try not to overdo it when you give your friend a makeover! Just a dab of lip gloss and a touch of blusher will give her a lovely, natural look.

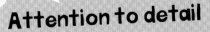

Attention to detail

Looking good is all about the details. Pick accessories that make the most of your clothes. Break up boring tops with a funky belt or team with a sparkly necklace.

Perfectly polished

Looking good isn't just about fashion – it's about taking care of your whole body, inside and out!

Choose your treats

Did you know that the good eating habits explained earlier can also affect your looks? If you want glowing skin and lovely hair, say 'no' to junk food. When you are hungry, choose fruit instead of crisps, and water instead of fizzy drinks.

Wonderful water

Your skin needs lots and lots of water! Drink plenty to keep it feeling soft. Wash your face in lukewarm water every morning and evening, using a clean towel to gently pat the skin dry.

Sun and sleep

Your skin is precious, so look after it well. Get enough beauty sleep every night – if you don't feel fresh, your skin won't look fresh! In hot weather, use sun cream and wear a sun hat to protect your skin.

Hair food

A good diet will help to keep your hair shiny and healthy, too. Foods like meat, fish, cheese and eggs are full of protein – just the stuff for glossy, shiny hair.

Good hair day

Be kind to your hair! Brush it well every day, and have regular trims at the hairdresser's. This will stop you getting split ends and keep your hair in tip-top condition.

Salon secrets

1. Wash your hair regularly.
2. Always rinse your locks after swimming.
3. When you wash your hair, let it dry naturally sometimes.
4. If you have to use a hairdryer, dry your hair with a towel first.
5. Don't brush your hair when it's wet or it might stretch and break.

Freshen up

Do you like chilling out at the end of the day in a lovely hot bath? Care for your body from top to toe and let your natural beauty shine through!

Smelly stuff

Water is best for your skin when you bathe or shower – you don't need loads of soaps and products, however sweet they smell. Warm water will clean out tiny pores in your skin without blocking them up.

Sensitive skin

If you are muddy after playing outside, then you'll need to use some soap to get the dirt off! If your skin is sensitive, choose a mild soap and don't use too much of it.

Break a sweat

When you do something energetic, such as your favourite sport, you may get a bit sweaty. This doesn't have to be a problem – just put on some deodorant before you go out.

Handy hygiene

It's important to wash your hands during the day, especially before you eat, after going to the toilet and when you've played with your pet. Washing your hands stops germs from spreading.

Love those nails!

When you have a bath or shower, check your hands and clean your fingernails if you need to! Long, dirty fingernails don't look great, so try to file them so they stay neat.

Brush up

No one likes smelly breath, so make sure you don't have it. Clean your teeth every morning after breakfast, and every evening before bedtime. Have regular check-ups at the dentist, too.

Prepare to impress

Make time to get ready for special occasions.

- 1 hour before: take a bubbly bath
- 45 minutes before: dry your hair
- 30 minutes before: get dressed
- 20 minutes before: style or pin up hair
- 10 minutes before: add a touch of make-up
- 5 minutes before: spritz on your favourite perfume

Feeling good

Feeling happy helps you stay healthy. Even when you're super-busy with school and friends, try to make time to de-stress and unwind.

Don't worry!

Try not to worry too much. Worrying makes you sad and it can stop you sleeping well at night. When you're tired, you are more likely to catch a cold or get ill.

Talk about it

If something is bugging you, don't keep it a secret. Talking to someone will make you feel heaps better. Sharing a problem is the first step towards sorting it out.

Get some help

If a problem won't go away, talk to an adult you trust, for example your teacher or someone in your family. If you are being bullied, this person will be able to help you get things straightened out.

Stop the stress

If you are feeling stressed, stop what you are doing and do something else that you really enjoy. Play some sport or music, or make a fuss of your pet!

Wind down

We all need plenty of sleep so that we can grow and function properly. If you find it hard to doze off at night, make sure you unwind before you go to bed.

Just relax!

Some people relax best when they are with good friends. Others prefer to chill out on their own, perhaps reading quietly or listening to music. How do you relax?

Stress busters!

- ☺ take five deep breaths
- ☺ phone a caring friend
- ☺ step into the sunshine
- ☺ think of all your favourite things
- ☺ hug someone you love

Spoil yourself

'Me time' matters! If you don't stop and spoil yourself sometimes, you'll end up feeling worn out and fed up.

Get pampered

Make a date with your mates to have a girly pampering session. Try out some new make-up, paint your nails and do some homemade beauty treatments! Relax and have a good laugh together.

Sunita is invited to **Katie's** bedroom spa pampering session on Friday after school

Please bring your dressing gown and a hair brush

RSVP [No little brothers allowed!]

Cool as a cucumber

After a long day at school, lie on the sofa and shut your eyes. Rest a thin slice of cucumber on each eyelid – it's a great way to soothe and refresh your tired eyes.

Shop till you drop

If you really need cheering up, the only answer may be to hit the shops with a friend. Treat yourselves to a cake in a café, then blow your pocket money on something you've had your eye on for ages!

Happy faces

Give your best mate a facial massage. Smooth her forehead and cheeks with your fingertips, working in small circles. Be very gentle and try not to tickle!

Smells good

Are you bored with the bottle of perfume you got last birthday? Have a scent-swapping party – the best bit is trying out the perfumes and deciding which one you like best!

One-to-one

Ask your mum or dad to take you out somewhere, just the two of you. It doesn't have to be an expensive outing – you'll have fun being together, and doing something different for a change.

sleep tight

Everyone needs to sleep – even dynamic divas like you! Your body is growing, and that takes up loads of vital energy.

A good night's sleep

If you don't get enough sleep, you can become tired and grumpy. You might also find it difficult to work properly at school. You need about ten hours of sleep a night to stay healthy and happy.

Early night

It sounds obvious, but the easiest way to get more sleep is to go to bed earlier! On school days try to be an early bird, saving your late nights for the weekend.

Calm down

Choose to do calming things just before bedtime. Have a nice bath, and have a hot, milky drink. Don't do anything that makes your brain or body have to work too hard!

One last thing

Sometimes it's hard to get to sleep, but there can be good reasons for this. Give yourself time to wind down before you go to bed – don't play computer games or watch loud TV shows just before you turn out the light.

Bedtime story

Try to get into the habit of reading a relaxing book at bedtime. It can be a novel, short story or even one of your school subjects! You could listen to a talking book CD. You'll soon feel sleepy and ready to drop off.

Off to sleep

If you really can't get to sleep, stop worrying. That will only keep you awake longer. Instead, think about something completely different – like an A to Z list of all your favourite celebs!

Dreamer's dictionary

chocolate time for a treat
forest think something through
letter listen to your heart
party be more sociable
tunnel keep moving forwards

Happy and healthy quiz

Are you healthy inside and out? Get a notebook and write down the answers to this great lifestyle quiz.

1. What's the healthiest way to get to school?
   a share a lift
   b walk or cycle
   c take the bus

2. Which of these indoor sports will teach you to be fit and safe?
   a judo
   b chess
   c gymnastics

3. What's the best way to get into a new sport?
   a watch people playing it on telly
   b wait until a friend is interested in giving it a go
   c sign yourself up at your local sports club

4. Which girls' sport is even more popular than netball?
   a football
   b hockey
   c tennis

5. Which of these meals is it OK to miss?
   a breakfast
   b any meal, if you don't fancy it
   c you should never miss a meal

6. Which of these helps your skin?

   a fizzy drinks

   b junk food

   c water

7. If you're stressed, what's a good way to unwind?

   a play a computer game

   b take a long walk

   c eat a takeaway

8. How much sleep do you really need?

   a as little as you can get away with

   b about six hours a night

   c about ten hours a night

Look back at these pages: *Get fit!* (pages 4-5); *Indoor play* (pages 6-7); *Outdoor action* (pages 10-11); *Eat smart* (pages 12-13); *Perfectly polished* (pages 20-21); *Feeling good* (pages 24-25); *Sleep tight* (pages 28-29).

How well did you do?
Count your correct answers below to find out!

0-3 You're on the right track, but there's stacks more you can learn about how to stay happy and healthy.

4-6 Not bad! You've got a pretty clear idea of what's good for you and what isn't! Keep up the great work.

7-8 You're the best! You know just what to do to make sure you always look and feel amazing.

Quiz answers: 1. b, 2. a, 3. c, 4. a, 5. c, 6. c, 7. b, 8. c

Index